INTERESTING CHARACTERS
OF BYGONE LOWESTOFT

Remembered by
Geoffrey Brock

INTERESTING CHARACTERS OF BYGONE LOWESTOFT

First published 2013

'Yarnspinner' publications.

ISBN 987 0 9927327 0 7

ACKNOWLEDGEMENTS:

To Kayleigh Clarke for her illustrations.

To Maureen Long for her help in compiling this book.

To all the people who helped make this book possible

Typeset at Coachman's Cottage

Printed by Leiston Press, Leiston, Suffolk

INTRODUCTION

I wrote this little book about the more colourful inhabitants of Lowestoft in an attempt to recapture some of the flavour of years gone by – when colourful and eccentric people seemed to exist in the town in abundance.

The people in this book are taken from all periods of Lowestoft's history, and, in my view, offer as important an insight into a town's history as books on, for instance, architecture or industry.

Today, such 'characters' are few and far between; therefore I hope the reader is given a pleasant glimpse into former days by reading of some of their exploits.

Geoffrey Brock, October 2013

CONTENTS

ARTHUR

Arthur was a man often seen in times past about the streets of Lowestoft. At least by sight he was well–known to many. With large, protruding teeth and in appearance not unlike Leonard Rossiter (of Rising Damp fame) he was of rather advanced years. He wore an old brown overcoat and a Homburg hat, summer and winter alike, always walking with his hands clasped behind his back. A pocket–watch on a gold chain lived in his waistcoat. A long, red necktie accompanied the coat and he swayed slightly from side to side as he walked. No–one knew what his last name was – he was just Arthur.

He had a phenomenal memory. Once he had asked you your name he would remember it for good and on future meetings could always greet you by it. Quite a feat, considering he must have met and spoken to hundreds of people and then systematically remembered the name of each one. If you bought him a cup of tea he would be your friend for life – and alcohol even more so! He generally frequented the little cafés that used to abound in the back streets of the town, and quite often the pubs. Sometimes in summer he took his time – and a bottle – down on the sea–front to pass the time and wait, in pleasant surroundings, for the day to go by.

Considering the environment which he inhabited perhaps he was unusual. He was well–spoken and well–informed, could tell you everything about what was happening in the world – and indeed, talk about almost any subject under the sun. I think he had few real friends and probably sat alone in rooms, listening to the World Service long into the night, listening to the radio and reading; the only things for a highly intelligent and cultured man in an impoverished and solitary predicament.

Occasionally he would produce gold–rimmed glasses and a beautiful, leather–bound notebook and studiously write something down. Sometimes he would produce the notebook and pen in response to something you said. Personal effects such as these, refined and individualistic as in many ways was Arthur himself, seemed like him to be left over from better days.

He used to talk about his time in the war and about travelling and working abroad. He said that he had seen service abroad during the war and afterwards had worked in India. He had caught malaria during his time there and was hospitalised for a considerable time. When discharged he was unable to work and so had come back to England. He had become separated from his family.

He would tell you this much, but the rest of his life–story remained a mystery, even when he was very inebriated he said little. So where he came from or who he was no–one would ever really know. He had spent time in the Colonial Civil Service, this much we knew, because he gave one of his reasons for his being in England as 'they ran out of colonies, and I ran out of money.' So, ageing and with failing health, he had come to live in Lowestoft as he thought he would be better looked after in England but it was not so.

During his time in India he claimed to have met a Fakir, who had 'touched him with luck' and Arthur offered to pass on this magic to anyone whom he liked, which could be someone who bought him tea or a drink or indeed who found the time to talk to him, but Arthur's 'magic' needed to be taken with salt – and a good deal more than a pinch at that!

At times, particularly if inebriated, he would say to anyone he happened on, "I'm not fed up ya know old chap, no, not fed up at all, so if I look fed up now ya know – I'm not fed up – no, not at all." Over and over again he repeated this monologue, until you made your excuses and left.

Arthur was an enigma; one of those incongruous, improbable people who just seem to appear from time to time out of the wood and bricks around run–down old boarding–houses and back streets in towns such as Lowestoft.

I don't know quite what happened to Arthur. And neither, it seems, does anyone else. He definitely added something to life but I'm not sure quite what it was. I think he just faded away and drifted into some other incarnation. God rest his soul – wherever it may be!

ARTHUR SIZER

Apart from the war years, which he spent out in Burma and in other parts of the world, Arthur Sizer lived most, if not all, of his life in Lowestoft. His married life began in Corton however where, in his own choice turn of phrase, he 'grew many a cabbage.'

He had a mania for collecting wood and hours of his spare time would be spent walking on the beach in search of this natural commodity. Beachcombing led to his finding all manner of things, including huge planks and sleepers (which he would cart home balanced on his old trade–bike or on a two–wheeled cart) and the odd bomb or two left over from the war – which hopefully he did not! The back garden of his house in Avondale Road sported a huge pile of wood and myriad objects which had trawled themselves up from the ocean's depths during storms.

The 'Tip' consisted of a large concrete bay into which the public would come to dispose of anything within reason that they felt it necessary to dispose of and was located in Ness Point, former site of the old Beach Village and the most Easterly point in Britain. Today it's the site of Gulliver, our most Easterly new–age windmill.

With a simplicity lost in modern life people would deposit unwanted items in the concrete bay and other people, if they desired, were pretty much free to take them. There were bylaws prohibiting the taking of waste from the dump but they were rarely, if ever, enforced and in any event the dump area was unsupervised. Sizer's garden, the two big old sheds in it and also his house, were living testaments to the number of useful objects which people disposed of at the most Easterly point in Britain.

He had a flamboyant, theatrical streak, and his 'normal' mode of dress was reminiscent of an old–time longshore fisherman. Clad in 'sou'westers', oilskin jackets and suchlike, he attired himself in these be it summer or winter, regardless of temperature. Large in stature with a huge ginger beard, he cut a highly recognisable figure about the town. His beard went well with his Scottish outfit – he was particularly proud of this latter. From time to time he sported a tunic and plaid, a kilt, puttees and a sporran and a beret complete with cap–badge. He would boast that he had acquired all of this from charity shops. He would often wear outfits in several different combinations, sometimes wearing the kilt with a camouflage jacket, Wellington boots and a tin hat – and now and then he would also wear a wig and varnish his nails!

He frequently wore a wartime fireman's tin helmet with a carrier–bag stretched over it. Once someone was imprudent enough to ask him why he did this. "Ha," replied Sizer, "Helps stop the ole hat going rusty o' course" – his tone of voice conveying that he thought this should be obvious!

Quirky remarks from Sizer were a commonplace. Out in the yard at Brooke Marine where he worked he once drew the foreman to his shoulder, pointed up in the sky, and said, "Look, the clouds are all going the wrong way!"

On another occasion at Brooke Marine, a party of school–leavers were being shown around the yard and had reached the area where Sizer was working. "What do you want to do then, boy?" Sizer asked one member of the party. "Dunno," the boy replied, "Think I'd like to be a lorry–driver's mate." "That's all very well," replied Sizer, "but what if lorry–drivers don't want to be your mate, mate? What then? I suppose you'll end up working here!"

On another occasion, whilst eating a bag of chips, he remarked to someone, "The chips from this shop have improved since that Chinaman took over. They used to have little black things in 'em, but since he took over I haven't seen one little black thing in any of 'em!"

On yet another occasion, he was seen leaving the local D.H.S.S office, where he had apparently been to enquire about his pension. He obviously had not met with satisfactory service for he was shouting as he left, "My God – what would Cromwell have made of that bloody shower?"

8

If he saw what appeared to be a party of schoolchildren about the town, he would shout, "What's the best school in Lowestoft?" The children would naturally shout back the name of their own school with gusto!

Once, after seeing a busker at work, he bought a little plastic trumpet from Woolworth's and played it outside that celebrated (and now extinct) store. At the end of the session Sizer was in jubilant mood, due to having paid only 50p for the trumpet but making four pounds. "I wasn't even playing it properly!" he exclaimed.

He mysteriously acquired a small cat from somewhere and this cat he would walk out on a lead. This I know is not unheard of in the instance of Siamese cats but this particular cat was just an ordinary little tabby. The two of them would walk about together, the cat sometimes sitting on his shoulder, and when Sizer did his busking the cat would lay down at his feet, just like a dog! Then one day it seemed to vanish as abruptly as it had arrived.

He also appeared with a ukulele and referred to it as 'the littlest guitar in Christendom'. He appeared intermittently on several occasions with one or the other of his little collection of instruments and no doubt made 'a few quid'.

During his life Sizer had acquired quite a large number of antiques and curios, some of them worth quite a large amount of money. For instance, he used to collect Scrimshaws; (for those who don't know these were motifs carved in ivory, mainly from the tusks of walruses, by the crews of whaling vessels in order to occupy their spare time as they cruised the oceans in search of quarry). Thieves took a good number of these when they decided to break in and help themselves to his collection as well as several other valuable items.

Incensed by their actions, Sizer contrived a plan of campaign to prevent similar occurrences in future. Using electrical knowledge gleaned during his service in the Army he wired up the metal window frames in his house to the mains, so at the flick of a switch the windows sizzled with mains voltage electricity. No–one ever tried to burgle him again or the results might well have been interesting!

He always insisted on wearing his kilt, even in the coldest weather. Sizer claimed, "It hardens the legs," (which latterly, in cold weather, would often become chapped and blotched with chilblains.)

Sizer died in 1993, aged seventy–three. He was a good old boy – one who could see the funny side of life – a local version of Spike Milligan, perhaps? He liked to have a bit of fun and to make others laugh and his humour could be hilarious but also, despite all his play–acting and exhibitionism, he had something about him that was quite down to earth; and somehow reflected very well the life of old Lowestoft.

TOMMY THE 'SANDWICH–MAN'

Better known in Lowestoft than the Town Mayor at any given time (and probably far more popular), Tommy Turrell epitomized those long–gone days when fishing–boats thronged the harbour, brown and cream Corporation buses rolled through the town and charged pennies to ride in them, and shops were homely, wooden–fronted concerns which sold items loose, and weighed them in pounds and ounces on polished brass scales. He was born in about 1904 to a fishing family but Tommy was, in someone's words 'not quite the same as other folk'. Deemed unfit for a life at sea, instead he was pointed in the direction of an agricultural career – that of hoeing beet and performing a series of simple tasks on nearby farms. Tommy got along quite well with agricultural work and in this way he earned a living for several years.

This for whatever reason, either the agricultural work itself or his inclination to do it, dried up for Tommy after a certain point. His choice of other work was limited. After being for a time on what was then National Assistance, he managed to find employment with a small local firm which specialized in advertising. His job was to walk around the town displaying 'sandwich boards' as they were called. These were body size boards at front and rear, joined by leather shoulder–straps and displayed advertisements for various products. 'Sandwich–men' as they were known are rarely, if ever, seen these days and are a part of a bygone world but at the time they were a common enough sight.

Some of the products displayed on these men's boards gave rise to a certain irony, as the sandwich–men were of the poorest class of people and, as such, could afford to buy very little above survival level, whereas some of the products they advertised on their boards were expensive luxuries, which they had no hope of ever buying.

Largely due to his work as a sandwich–man which required him to walk around the town for most of the day, Tommy became a very well–known local figure. His characteristic, battered old Homburg hat, always worn on the side of his head, his quick, scuttling gait and his long old greatcoat were the distinctive marks which made him instantly recognizable. He also earned himself some extra cash by running errands between the shops and businesses in the area.

At various times, his sandwich boards proclaimed the virtues of anything and everything, from a religious tract to a type of boot polish, to the latest Rolls–Royce; everything took pride of place on his boards at some time or another.

Even when it snowed he would often soldier on with his boards and boys coming out of school would sometimes hurl snowballs at the boards for fun, until there were so many snowballs festooning them that it was impossible to read that which was advertised there!

Previously living with his mother in the Beach Village, after her death Tommy went to live at a boarding–house in London Road South. He was there for some time but when war broke out he was evacuated to the workhouse at Ditchingham. The workhouse there had been colonized by the war effort but only shortly before had still been in use as a workhouse. It is perhaps worth mentioning here that some workhouses were operational after World War Two – and even into the 1950s! Ditchingham, however, ceased to perform this function some time before the war, and stood empty until it was taken into use as a billet for land–girls and various others such as Tommy, who needed to stay there for the duration of the war.

Tommy again found himself hoeing beet on the adjacent farm and carried on throughout the war, hardly aware I would imagine that it was taking place and no doubt enjoying the company of the land–girls! Tommy, it is likely, had a 'good' war.

After the war he moved back to Lowestoft and went to stay at the same boarding–house he had occupied before, for a while taking a job at a local fruitier, putting fruit and vegetables into boxes and helping to unload lorries, which he hated.

After this he managed to get a job with a newly–opened Gents' Outfitters in the town who were promoting their wares. Dressed in the finest clothes and even wearing a top hat, he was billed 'Tommy the Toff'. He loved playing this role and for a while 'Tommy the Toff' became his nickname around the town.

For years he was active in the Salvation Army. In the latter part of his life he was deemed one of their longest–serving members. It is interesting to note that his membership of the Army originated from the time when a member who was collecting in the street drew his attention to a religious tract he was displaying. He suggested that if he came to their centre he and the other members would give him tea and teach him the true Word of God. Later in life, he would not only attend their service each Sunday but those of three other churches as well!

When Christmas was approaching he looked forward to it with the breathless excitement of a child. He would announce loudly to anyone who happened to be passing, in broad Suffolk dialect, all the lovely things he would be doing to celebrate this glorious event. "I'm a–goin' to St Margaret's Church, and they're a–gonna let me ring the Christamas bells! Then there's the Carol Service – and then, all a–bein' well, we'll be a–havin' a party, jelly an' cakes an' crackers an' a big ole Christamas cake! I wish you could be there, Sir, I just wish you could be there!" he would say.

As the Carnival was held in August, Tommy had something to look forward to for most of the year. When the time was drawing near for this event, usually a couple of months before the parade, he would tell passers–by, again with considerable excitement, that he was going to be in the Carnival. As something of a local celebrity he was given the seat of honour – that of riding next to the Carnival Queen. This, of course added to the general excitement. "I'm a–gonna be on the front float, a–sittin' next to the Carnival Queen!"

Each August, when the day of the parade arrived, floats bedecked with colour, strangeness, lights and pageantry, moved slowly through the town and Tommy could not contain his excitement. The Great Day had come at last and there he would be, sitting just as he had said, on the front float up beside the Carnival Queen, dressed in some costume or other (he must have worn an infinite variety over the years) and waving to the crowds for all he was worth. As he made abundantly clear, this was always one of the most enjoyable days in his year.

He told one interviewer that he would like to be in the Carnival 'for ever and ever' and this, at least indirectly, has come true for him. In 1985 the Carnival Committee had a trophy made in his name. From then on the 'Tommy Turrell Shield' was to be awarded for Best Adult Carnival Exhibit.

After many years, the time came when Tommy grew old and feeble and went to live at 'Wilmington', a home for the elderly in The Avenue, Pakefield, where in summer he could be seen sitting outside in the sun. At eighty he was now too infirm to take part in the procession but did not miss it as it assembled almost outside where he lived, the organizers, much to their credit, having re–routed it for this very purpose. Tommy enjoyed his twilight years at 'Wilmington' and was very popular with the staff there. He eventually died in 1988 at the age of eighty–three. Perhaps, somewhere beyond the stars, his wish has come true and there is a celestial Carnival in which he rides – for ever and ever.

DON ROUT, AN ARTIST, OF PAKEFIELD

Don Rout, a man who came to be just about the most eccentric and colourful artists in the area, was born in Burnham Thorpe, Norfolk, in 1931.

On leaving school he decided that post–war Britain was a pretty dull affair so he took himself off across the continent with his guitar, busking and sometimes doing odd jobs such as grape–picking to get by. "They didn't really understand busking in Morocco," remarked Don. There he had to work in a series of filthy kitchens in order to make ends meet. Returning to England after two years, penniless and burned brown by the sun, he decided that he should find work and as a result started as a trainee marine biologist for the Ministry of Agriculture and Fisheries, whose laboratory was housed in the recently refurbished Empire Hotel, which stands on Pakefield cliff.

On first arriving in the area, Don lodged with a Mrs Howard whose son incidentally also worked at the 'Lab', as they termed it. Some time later when finances allowed he acquired a bungalow in West Grove, Pakefield. Now having the space to indulge in his natural creativity, Don painted wall–murals throughout the interior, including the ceiling, made models, painted numerous pictures and filled the rest with the trinkets and artefacts collected magpie–like from charity shops and jumble–sales. Before long, his mother came to stay, Don's father having recently died and she wanted to be with her family. She also had a daughter living in nearby Southwold.

Whilst not on duty at the 'Lab', as well as indulging in his passion for painting, Don was an avid collector of blues and folk records. With a good singing voice and a confederate, Bob Burns, he strummed his way around the local pubs and clubs. Don once remarked that the very first time he ever earned money for a gig was in London, playing outside a Lyons coffee–house, total remuneration two pounds. The pair became quite popular in the area, not only for their musical abilities but also for their humorous repertoire.

Don continued to paint and, as he became better known in the area, his main venue for exhibitions became the Theatre Centre in Morton Road, Pakefield – now the Seagull Theatre. As well as frequently staging exhibitions there Don joined in heartily with the other activities taking place and took part in some of the plays and musical venues, and in making and painting scenery for the players. Years later, a mural which he painted of fish–porters going about their work on Lowestoft Fish Market still adorns one of the walls there.

Although Don was born and brought up in Burnham Thorpe with its striking classical Norfolk countryside, his painting reflected little or nothing of such a background; it did not inspire him as it has done so many other painters. When his work was commented on he replied, "My paintings are what they are, explanations are pretty irrelevant really. The main thing is, people look at them and they either 'get it' and feel drawn into the painting or they don't."

His work at the 'Lab' continued to supply Don with a wealth of experiences. Voyaging on board the Ministry research vessel was at first a new experience in itself for Don, who before joining the Ministry, in his own words had 'never had more than a day at the seaside.' Some of the places that the Ministry vessel visited for the sake of science were fascinating and included the Arctic Circle, which he found the most fascinating of all.

His first sighting of the Northern Lights created an impression which was etched on his mind for the rest of his life and some of the strange marine creatures which he dealt with as a Marine Biologist influenced his perception of nature and of life itself; all were woven into the strange and exotic tapestry of his art.

After a while, Don moved house and purchased a large ground–floor flat in nearby Florence Road, joking that he had moved because it was slightly nearer

to the pub. This flat sported particularly high ceilings and after living there for some time Don, having accrued everything under the sun, decided that in order to make more space he had to take advantage of this fact – build upwards as it were. So one day he drafted in some work colleagues and between them they built a contraption; a collection of huge platform–shelves running almost to the height of the ceiling. On these shelves Don stashed his numerous and varied collection of objects and slept in the space underneath in a strange four–poster bed affair.

This arrangement proved satisfactory for several years until in the middle of one night, eventually succumbing to accumulated weight, the whole lot suddenly collapsed to a deafening crash, trapping the recumbent Don in his 'four–poster'. His mother, who was sleeping in the next bedroom, could do little to free him as she was an elderly lady. Neither was there anyone else available to help as this happened in the small hours of the morning.

Don, quite unconcerned as was his nature, simply went back to sleep in his pit under the fallen debris until a later hour when help could be summoned. Called in off the street by Don's anxious mother, three men, complete strangers, lifted masses of accumulated objects and broken shelving away, thus releasing Don from his prison, shared a cup of tea after the job was done and went on their way amid much jollity. Needless to say, Don's sleeping arrangements changed somewhat after this episode!

Don's work at the 'Lab' continued, as did his flamboyant sense of humour. One day a dressmaker's dummy, resplendent in strange garb, appeared in his work–space. When asked about it he replied that he was lonely working on his own. "I needed some company and she can't answer back," said Don.

Meanwhile Don, with Bob Burns, continued to give live performances in the area. By this time they had amassed a band and a real bunch of hearties they were too! Bearded and artily dressed, they endeavoured to drink the pub dry whilst playing old favourites, blues and folk, and old pub songs, filled with humour (some slightly bawdy), and always got a laugh. *Maggie May*, *Sweet Violets*, and an endless repertoire of other old favourites filled the air.

There was a woman, Sheila, who played the flute and Derek, an artist and inventor, who was partly earning a living by constructing a massive glass–fibre giant outside a workshop at Kessingland. This giant was over twenty feet high, surrounded by scaffolding, and over the years has become a feature of Botton Brothers Pleasure Beach in Great Yarmouth for whom it was constructed. There was also a Jack, considerably smaller in size, but he was stolen. Derek also constructed a double–bass which appeared to work quite well and was apparently made from the glass–fibre hub of a boat's propeller! Bob Burns played guitar. Another chap played banjo and mandolin and Don himself played guitar and other odds and ends such as the penny whistle and the ukulele.

I used to go and watch them perform at the *Trowel and Hammer* in Pakefield Street. At the time (the early '70s) it was run by an old couple called Ted and Kit Thacker – and was a real old fishermen's pub, probably largely unchanged for the last two hundred years, with rugged wooden panelling, a shove–halfpenny board, a ring–board and various other old games; old wooden settles on which to sit, a lovely open fireplace which burned logs – all things rarely seen today. Don's musical sessions often attracted some weird characters, including a man who always wore a white robe and sandals. He claimed that he could put himself into hypnotic trances at will and sitting in the woods become at one with the trees, impervious to weather conditions and able to go without food for months. Even he was not the weirdest. At gatherings such as this people with esoteric leanings and theories seemed to be everywhere!

After twenty years of service Don was forced to leave his work with the Ministry, due to ill–health, and I gather that he missed the stimulus that his work and the company of work–colleagues provided but he still seemed to draw plenty of inspiration from somewhere. One of his gifts was being able to talk to anyone about any subject under the sun, from spirituality and philosophy and the deeper meaning of life to the most mundane everyday tittle–tattle. He was a mine of information; people often consulted him on rare flora or fauna or any natural phenomena that they might have found and he was often able to come up with the answers.

One of Don's more striking creations was his driftwood aeroplane. An abstract representation of a World War I fighter–bomber, he constructed it together with one Bruce Lacy, an old friend, from driftwood the pair collected from the beach. Lacy was in his element with such ideas. An artist who also performed community theatre, he had made several representative sculptures in the past, as had Don. They constructed the aeroplane in the grounds of the Seagull Theatre. When it was finished it was transported, on none other than an open–topped bus, brightly painted and owned by one of their colleagues, to Barsham where the Medieval Fayre was about to take place, as it did every year during the 1970s.

The Fayre was an unusual event which included, amongst other things, fire–eaters, jugglers, musicians and, of course, a beer–tent selling real ale. The Fayre was full of strangely–garbed folk, dogs, tents and children; people arrived in old vans daubed with brightly–coloured designs and when it was dark lit fires from forest wood, played music and roasted a whole pig over a spit. Later, Don would take part in one of the Druidic rituals that Bruce Lacy and his wife and others travelled the country performing in fringe theatre but for the time–being Messrs Rout and Lacy and the driver of the bus parked their plane in a clearing and went off to the beer–tent.

After the Fayre at Barsham with its colourful hurly–burly had reached its end the aeroplane was carted back to Pakefield beach, where it had begun life in the form of driftwood and other miscellaneous detritus useful in the construction of such a model. Amazingly, it stayed intact for months on the beach, untouched by vandals, and passers–by out for a walk would stop to admire it and take pictures. Eventually when winter came, high winds and tides reduced it to its original components which, as artists, was just what its creators wanted!

Don decided to take up gardening and the way in which he approached it was very much a reflection of his character. He rented a nearby allotment and there soon appeared on it an array of stone circles and statues. Also there on an old garden bench was the dressmaker's dummy, which a while ago had accompanied Don in his work, this time clad in a pair of sunglasses and a straw hat. A particularly bold stone circle made from boulders which he took from the beach marked the middle of the ground. Here Don constructed a great pyramid of earth which probably took months of work to complete. Growing down the sides of this pyramid were all manner of vegetables which, to give Don his due, looked healthy and thriving. This was typical of Don. Whatever he tackled, he had to 'do different'.

In studies of ancient Egypt, he had acquired the idea that plants would grow better if in the vicinity of a pyramid–shape. Whether or not there is any truth in this theory I have no idea but the vegetables which grew there certainly thrived, and were considerably larger than average. Although frequently asked, Don would never really divulge the secret of these extra large plants and just used to say, "If I told you what it was, you wouldn't believe me." The whole layout of this piece of ground was so unique that it became legendary in the area and people would peer over the gate, musing at the spectacle. Like the aeroplane it must have graced many a photo album!

Don's work in his art continued and, if anything, he became more prolific and his paintings larger with the use of bolder colours. Branching out into sculpture he sculpted usually from plaster of Paris and curiously, although his paintings were generally very abstract, the sculptures were generally straight copies of natural things. For example one of the sculptures was a model of the three parts of a lupin seed, greatly enlarged, and also made from plaster of Paris. As a student of such phenomena he wanted people to see aspects of nature which lent themselves to aesthetic shapes but were often too small to be seen with the naked eye. He had a great dislike of critics although they gave him a measure of publicity and at one of his exhibitions told a reporter from a local

16

newspaper, "There's too much baloney talked about art appreciation. If you can't paint, the thing to do is become a critic!"

In the meantime he decided to take up *Tai Chi*, the Chinese art of fitness and self–defence, and could be seen performing all sorts of bodily contours and gesticulations in the name of this ancient and celebrated art – usually on the nearby beach and much to the curiosity, and sometimes prejudice, of the unenlightened. He once had cause to use the self–defence aspect of *Tai Chi* he said when attacked while out late at night by two ruffians who soon made off, utterly defeated when Don's demonstration of the martial arts was directed at them. He enacted his own sun worshipping ceremony which he performed with much gusto and chanting at every dawn, and when the sunset came he would enact the ceremony again. He also paid homage to the phases of the moon in much the same way. Don had a great love of the beach and the sea and as well as engaging in worshipping the phases of the sun and moon would spend all the time he could there, usually doing his painting when weather permitted, or creating natural sculptures out of driftwood and other assorted detritus he found there.

Possibly, at least part of his motive in constructing the sun–temple was to bait a trap for the nearby church. At any rate, what happened was that members of the aforesaid organisation had seen Don in his worship and, completely misconstruing the situation, had tried to take out a court injunction against him for devil–worship. The subsequent investigation was soon overturned and Don reacted with considerable mirth, telling the tale over and over again in the local pub. He loved exposing people's ignorance and bigotry so, although he never admitted as much, it is very likely that this was his motive; it was well in keeping with his mischievous sense of humour.

Death came suddenly for Don at the relatively early age of sixty–one. Still engaging in activities at the Seagull Theatre, he was taking part in one of the Alternative Cabaret nights that the Seagull held every so often – a show in November. Made up to look like a statue, his act was to stand stock still for some time whilst other activities were taking place on stage and then suddenly change position. It had been successful in other shows and Don could carry it off so that it created quite an impression. This time, however, back in the dressing–room he was complaining of stabbing pains in the chest. Refusing offers from various people to telephone for medical help, in spite of feeling unwell he went on to complete the rest of the show and then went home.

Next day, those that knew him heard that Don had died during the night. He was discovered by his mother to whom it must have been a terrible shock; he was thought to have died during the early hours of that morning.

People were very shocked and saddened for Don was generally well–liked in the community in which he lived, but later there was a general consensus that although sad that he had died at least one of the last things he did was something he loved, which was taking part in a performance. He was buried soon after at Kirkley cemetery, to a packed congregation. It was 1992.

Later that year, the Seagull held a special 'Don Rout Evening', and the spark of creative genius that Don had added to an area like Pakefield was commemorated. There was a poetry reading and an exhibition of Don's paintings and other creations. Members of the theatre enacted a play illustrating Don's unusually colourful life and the theatre was packed with the people who had known him.

On the cliffs at Pakefield there are a number of wooden benches, donated in commemoration by people who felt that this or that individual had given something special to the area during their lives. On one of these the brass plaque reads 'DON ROUT WAS HERE 1931–1992' – summing up perfectly in a few simple but well–chosen words the man that I knew.

SHELLEY COOKE – A DWARF NOTORIOUS!

"You have been in this court almost as many times as there are days in the year and it is always for some deed related to the misuse of alcohol" – this comment being directed by the judge at one Shelley Butcher Cook, the man featured in our story, yet again in the dock at the local Magistrates Court. On this occasion he was convicted of being drunk and disorderly in a public place and fined ten shillings. Cook at this time was sixty–four years of age and hitherto had led a rather colourful life.

Born into a Lowestoft Beach family in 1810 he was the youngest of five boys and three girls, none of whom as far as we know shared his exceptionally small stature. Perhaps it is interesting at this stage to note that he appears to have taken his middle name, Butcher, from the distaff side of his family as many people appear to have done in those days.

The most obvious thing about Shelley was his size – or I should say lack of it – he stood only four feet tall. Being this small certainly appears to have been a major influence in his life and, indirectly at least, seems to have led him to adopt his precarious lifestyle.

Because he was so tiny he was often the butt of jibes by his classmates but was strong and athletic for his size and could respond well with his fists as more than one teasing schoolboy found to his cost!

In winter when the frosts came he could often be found ice skating on the surrounding broads and dykes. He was an accomplished ice skater and, although his short legs did not permit him to run to any extent on the ice, his speed and prowess was a match for anyone.

If anything Shelley's troubles increased on leaving school. Because of his small size employment was difficult to find. His brothers were all fishermen and his father had a successful career in the merchant service but the community in which Shelley lived provided very little he could successfully do. Eventually he found an apprenticeship with a Mr Palmer, a shoemaker. He worked for Palmer for a while and proved himself to have an aptitude for the trade but Cook began to drink, so much so that he lost his apprenticeship and became unemployable.

According to Shelley it was Palmer, his employer, who introduced Shelley to drink in the first place. Palmer was a Strict Baptist and on Sundays he would preach at the local church, taking Cook with him. Shelley, who had a good musical ear, had the duty of 'setting hymns and starting the tune' and, surprisingly for his size, he sang in a deep, baritone voice.

Because of his short legs Shelley usually had difficulty in completing the return journey and on the way home one Sunday night Shelley as usual complained of fatigue so Palmer promised him, "Never mind, in future we'll take my pony trap but let's wet your whistle with a pint of porter when we get to the *Crown*." After this episode the two of them visited the *Crown* on a regular basis when returning home from church. From that time on Shelley developed a taste for drink which was to remain with him for most of his life and eventually lead to his death.

After his brief spell at the shoemaker's Shelley does not appear to have worked again. Wandering the cobbled streets of the town he frequented the pubs and beer shops that abounded at the time. (A beer–shop consisted of little more than the front parlour of a private dwelling which had been given over to selling cheap beer. Few regulations were required in order to set one up and as they were highly profitable they had become numerous and were often squalid and tawdry). During this time Shelley collected a litany of appearances and fines too numerous to mention individually, most of which were connected with the excessive consumption of alcohol. He was naturally a fighter and when he had been drinking his more common offences seemed to be causing an affray, being drunk and disorderly, assault, and damage to property.

He seemed to have a talent for throwing a whole public house into a brawl at a moment's notice and he was constantly being removed by police to spend a night (or longer) in the cells. However, one incident for which he appeared in court was the result of a stupid prank played on him by one of his contemporaries. When he got up to buy a drink in one of the 'spit and sawdust' establishments in which he spent most of his time, someone decided to pack gunpowder into his pipe and then place the tobacco on top. When he lit the pipe there was suddenly a loud report and the air was full of blasted clay – the pipe had exploded into a thousand fragments, breaking the window above where he sat. Shelley, who could well have been injured, was (unjustly) charged with causing an explosion in a public place and the wilful damage of property. This episode found him in prison for two months.

He continued on in this precarious and itinerant lifestyle, spending some time with the colony of tramps that inhabited the area situated on Corton cliffs, which became known as Tramps'Alley. Here the tramps gathered, lighting fires on the beach and sleeping in the woods and perhaps it is interesting to note that although this area is now a nudist beach, it derived its name from the stalwart tramps of Victorian England! Shelley lived by 'pooling his lot' with the tramps and all chipped in to buy food and alcohol which they shared. In town, Shelley would scrounge a drink or two from the local fishermen who, more often than not, were more than happy to get him drunk for their amusement.

The only time he seems to have been offered work seems have been when the travelling fairs came to the Lowestoft and then it was always as a freak in a sideshow or as a clown. "The first offer I had was from a woman who was as big as a mountain," said Shelley. "She offered me ten shillings a week and promised to treat me well." The offers were always declined except for one from Tom Thumb, who he met and made friends with one summer when the fair was visiting. It was not clear exactly what transpired but at any rate Shelley ended up staying in Lowestoft, probably to the chagrin of the local magistrates to whom he continued to make himself a nuisance with his drunken and boisterous behaviour.

Given his tiny size it is a point of humorous speculation as to how he managed to see over the top of the witness box but for Cook court appearances continued to be a frequent occurrence! The years passed and Shelley's life seems to have continued in much the same pattern. Unfortunately for him he came to be the butt of humour for the ignorant or, as someone remarked, 'rough jokes for rough people'. The pranks played on him included being stripped of his clothes, covered in treacle and then thrown out in the street. On another occasion he was grabbed, beer was poured down his throat and, thus intoxicated, he was he was sewn up in a sack and left in the front porch of a house in London Road South. On yet another occasion he was stuffed into a hamper and put on a stagecoach bound for Norwich with a placard around his neck announcing him as 'A natural curiosity!' Luckily the hamper was intercepted and its contents released before the coach could begin its journey to Norwich or one might have wondered just what the staff at the Norfolk and Norwich Hotel might have made of this particular delivery!

The passage of time saw Shelley fall under the auspices of the Board of Guardians. Excessive poverty in those days was treated almost as a crime and if any person was found sleeping rough without the necessary penny to redeem them from a vagrancy order they would be put into the workhouse and this happened to Shelley. But unlike most workhouse inmates who toiled in misery, Shelley actually seemed to enjoy his visits there and even encouraged the police to 'run him in' for vagrancy by putting on a conspicuous show of begging!

Arriving for the first time at the Mutford and Lothingland Union Workhouse, he found that, "They gave me only light duties to do, if at all, and yet they still fed me." Shelley would be detained at the workhouse for a short time for each episode of vagrancy and then released, only to be pitched back into the endless cycle of brawls and run–ins that characterised his lifestyle.

Even for Cook however life was not without its lighter moments. He was still physically fit and, when the grip of winter came, in periods of sobriety he would demonstrate his prowess on the ice by somersaulting, skating round objects at lightning speed or simply winning races. The advent of the summer season brought Shelley some new forms of entertainment and also the chance to make himself some money.

In the latter half of the nineteenth century the seaside holiday was born. People had started to visit Lowestoft and other seaside towns, staying at the boarding houses along the sea–front which were rapidly expanding in numbers and spending their time in a way which was regarded as healthy and pleasurable. Shelley soon realised that not only did they have money to spend but were also somewhat gullible so he set about entertaining them in such a way that would part with some of their cash to his advantage.

A competent swimmer he would approach holidaymakers on the beach, offering to bet them that he could retrieve this object or that from the ocean bed. As his diminutive size gave the lie to his diving abilities they would nearly always take him up on the bet being sure, as Cook craftily anticipated, that they would win. Cook could dive to over two fathoms and sometimes won quite substantial sums of money in this fashion. He also entertained with some of the tricks that Tom Thumb had taught him during their time together. Flamboyantly dressed in a costume which Tom had made for him, he wheeled somersaults and performed handstands and acrobatics. He was also a competent juggler and, lying on a mat on the beach, he performed with both hands and feet, much to the applause of the crowds and money rained into his hat at the end of each act.

One of the more memorable escapades performed by Cook and related by those who witnessed it for some years to come happened as follows. A large schooner, the *Nymph*, had docked in what is now known as the yacht basin and Shelley, seeing it there, decided to play a prank. Shinning up the full height of the mainmast that towered up into the sky, he proceeded to shout until a crowd gathered on the pier near where the schooner was moored.

When a large crowd had gathered he launched himself off the top gallant back stay (a pole which runs at an angle from the mast and is then fixed to the deck) and, with a battle cry, slid like lightning the full length of the stay down to the deck, terrifying captain, crew and onlookers alike. "I came down like thunder to the belaying–pin," exclaimed Shelley, "and I could smell fire – my clothes were burned and my arms scorched by the rapid rate at which I came down. I don't know who was the most frightened, myself, or those who witnessed it," said Shelley.

Those who knew him always said that Shelley's drinking habits became less pronounced after he was released from the workhouse or from prison and then gradually increased until they spiralled out of control. On his last release from the workhouse however, a marked deterioration was seen in him, he was drinking more than ever and from always managing to be dapper and neatly dressed, his clothes were now in rags. Shelley at sixty–four years of age was now in the autumn of his life, his health had deteriorated and he had developed a hacking cough that usually marked the beginning of tuberculosis or a related illness. After a while he went to stay with his sister who lived locally. He was penniless, having long since spent any money he might have earned that summer but then, just when it seemed there was no hope for the little man, fortune smiled on him.

A Mr Livock, a local artist who knew Cook, offered him a way out of his plight. On condition that he stopped drinking, Livock was to paint his portrait and then charge the public one penny per head to see the painting. As Livock was an accomplished artist he surmised that by this means he might be able to raise sufficient funds for Cook's needs. The money was to go to pay for treatment for Shelley's condition (all medical treatment was charged for in those days), and to buy him good, healthy food and fit him out in decent clothing. This was all on the condition that Shelley abstained from alcohol – and in Livock's words, "Drank nothing stronger than ginger ale."

All having been agreed on, Shelley arrived at Livock's High Street studio and several hours (and laborious sittings) later a painting began to emerge which, when completed generally came to be regarded as a masterpiece. Posed in the cap and waistcoat which he always wore, Shelley was depicted sitting on an 18–gallon cask and clutching a pipe in one hand and a half–pint flagon in the other. Livock had managed to completely capture the stance and essential character of the notorious dwarf. He entitled the painting 'THE INTENDED TEMPLAR. MANY A TIME, MY BOYS, FULL TO THE BUNG!'

The local magistrates soon grasped the situation and decided to turn it to their advantage. Issuing an edict that anyone, be they publican or private individual known to supply Cook with any alcoholic beverage would be fined ten shillings, equally rewarding anyone who could supply information leading to a conviction. A poster bearing this information was distributed around the town, thus making it impossible for Cook to obtain alcohol.

As interest in the painting grew so the fund of pennies accrued and there were soon more than enough to outfit Shelley in a fine suit of clothes. He was also able to eat better (for a tiny man he had an astonishing appetite) and the medicine he was able to buy cleared up his chest infection.

A reformed character he soon started to attend the Baptist Chapel again, sitting next to none other than Mr Palmer, his old employer. Palmer was surprised and delighted to see him back in church and they soon rekindled their old friendship. Shelley started to ride in Palmer's pony trap and they even resumed their stop at the *Crown*. It seemed like old times, the only but perhaps significant difference being that Shelley's flagon now contained only ginger ale.

Because Shelley was a reformed character and had remained so for quite an appreciable time, it came as a shock to the people of Lowestoft to learn of his sudden death, apparently from alcoholic intoxication. Having been ejected from the *Crown* earlier in the evening for the sort of behaviour that usually results from drunkenness, he was found sitting on a wall outside in a semi–conscious state by two lads who happened to be passing and they trundled him in a wheelbarrow back to his sister's home in Clapham Road where he was staying.

This was about 9.30 on the evening of October 10th. His sister made him comfortable on the settee downstairs and went to bed. She had been worried about him because he had seemed in such a state and when she woke in the small hours of the morning and went to check if he was all right, Shelley was discovered to be dead.

His corpse was conveyed to the mortuary (which in those days was situated at the back of Pier Terrace, on the site now occupied by SLP Engineering and was conveniently situated near a small ice factory behind the present–day bridge control) in preparation for the inquest which took place on October 15th.

The inquest was held at the *Fox and Hounds*. Before the Bench were a jury of fifteen, a motley crew consisting mainly of fishermen who had drifted in and out of the *Crown* at various times on the evening that Cook had died, Mr Livock the artist and Cook's sister, Mary Welham. Mrs Welham testified that on the day that Cook died he had seemed listless and unwell and she thought that his health might be deteriorating again. She observed that when he got up that morning and attempted to walk to the bottom of the yard in order to wash and shave, he had difficulty in doing so. However, towards the evening she said he seemed considerably brighter and at about 7pm had taken his Bible and said that he was going to the Baptist Church. He went out and the next thing she knew was that at 9.30pm there was a knock on the door and Cook was delivered in a dishevelled state. She made sure he was comfortable downstairs and went off to bed. When she got up to check on him, to her shock she found that he had died. Why he had ended up at the *Crown* when he had said that he was going to the Baptist Church, and moreover returned home in such an intoxicated state, would forever remain a mystery to her.

Two fishermen, John Tracy and Jack Harding, testified that they had walked into the *Crown* on that Wednesday evening at about 9pm and Cook had been there. Harding, a big man with a shock of red hair, had asked him whether he could drink another bottle of ginger ale and Cook, who had seemed in high spirits but sober, had replied, "My boy, tonight I could drink twenty!" Harding had then bought him a bottle of ginger ale and they all chatted pleasantly for a while.

When the two bade their goodbyes Cook had still seemed normal but there were a group of men who entered as they were leaving, and clustered round the bar, conversing boisterously and buying drinks. Neither Tracy nor Harding recognised any of them and agreed that it was feasible that they might have procured alcohol for him, or spiked his drink. "It would not surprise me," added Tracy, "I have known men to grab him and on several occasions pour beer down his throat in order to get him drunk." He went on to say, "There were some boats in from away and I think they were the crew from one of them; they were Scottish I believe. Shelley used to cadge all his drinks as he never had any money. He used to do all right out of the boys from away but that was before he stopped drinking."

Mr Livock said he had known Cook for many years and thought him well able to cope with his rough and itinerant lifestyle. He said he admired Cook and thought him plucky so, when he got into dire straits he tried to help him. He went on to relate the story of the painting and said that when Cook stayed off drink and out of trouble for a long period he thought he had succeeded.

The District Coroner testified that an autopsy had been carried out and had revealed nothing medically amiss with Cook.

The general consensus came to be that Cook had started out with the intention of remaining sober but in the course of the evening had mysteriously become intoxicated. It was of course assumed that someone had 'spiked' his drink but there was no proof of this. In the summing–up the jury delivered a verdict of 'death by intoxication'.

Shelley's funeral took place on 18th October 1875, with masses of flowers by the graveside. All the local fisher–folk gathered to give him a send–off (including I suppose the hypocrites who had made his life a misery by persistently playing pranks on him and making him a laughing–stock) and thus the funeral marked the end of a true local character.

FROM RAGS TO RICHES AND BACK AGAIN –

THE STORY OF GEORGE COLE

A tall old man who always wore an immaculately starched apron he would, in the summer months, stretch himself out in an old lounge–chair, reading or passing the time of day with anyone who cared to stop and talk. Situated at the top of Pakefield Street, in the area which as since anyone can remember has been known as Pakefield Tramway the 'Emporium', or George's Junk Shed as the locals were wont to call it, was open to all who cared to enter and see what new acquisitions it might hold.

Sooner or later one would grow curious enough to pass beyond the large wooden doors and, with eyes grown accustomed to the dim light within, a veritable Aladdin's cave of objects, many from days gone by, old and obscure, would be seen and this was one of the fascinations.

There were old dressers, toilet pans and cisterns, black old stoves, tables, bicycles, chairs, oil lamps, road–lamps, washstands, fishing rods, mangles, pictures in frames, pictures not in frames, brass stands, brasses from horse–harness, horse–harness without brasses, battered musical instruments, pots, pans, stained–glass windows, old brass pumps and several unidentifiable objects – all with that elusive magic!

The first thing you would notice as you entered the 'Emporium' would be the trunk of a tree growing up through the earthen floor. When George constructed the building, a Victoria plum tree lay directly in its path. Not having the heart to destroy it, he constructed the roof of the building around its trunk and each autumn when the tree fruited the whole area outside would be showered with falling plums, to which George would invite people to help themselves.

Born in 1896 into an East End family, George worked with his father, a jobbing builder, learning all aspects of the trade and becoming a competent hand at all the skills needed in building. All this would stand him in good stead in later years, but for the time being he had other ambitions.

After a few years he left employment with his father and signed up as a boy sailor with the Royal Navy. George showed himself to be a competent seaman and, after a relatively short time, he rose to the rank of Chief Petty Officer and spent most of his time serving on cruisers.

During World War One, as a senior seaman, he was selected as one of a series of teams who were sent on various special missions by the Royal Navy. These teams were known as Prize Crews and one of the missions in which George found himself participating was transporting captured Turkish vessels to Great Britain.

Desiring change in 1928 George signed out of the Navy, moved back to London and set himself up as a builder. From small beginnings he built up a business – and did better than he could ever have imagined. Before long the humble terrace he had occupied in the East End was exchanged for a huge, detached house in the suburbs of Brighton and George was busily living it up on his new–found wealth.

Dining at the Ritz was now a frequent occurrence for him, as was shopping at Harrod's store or attending the Ascot races. Generally speaking, he was experiencing the exclusive lifestyle enjoyed only bythe very rich. The business continued to flourish and George to enjoy his new–found riches and all that went with them.

His company was responsible for a large proportion of the expansion of the suburbs from London out towards Brighton. As the business grew, George had a huge amount of capital laid out in property, and was borrowing money to invest in still more. The firm also owed thousands of pounds to building suppliers. However, turnover was good and there seemed to be no real problems. It was the recession, however, which occurred toward the end of the 1930s and seemed to happen almost overnight, which brought about the demise of George's company. The slump which hit Britain brought with it a corresponding, sudden drop in property prices. George was unable to extend loans to keep the company functioning and any property he attempted to sell was worth a fraction of its former value.

The company attempted various measures but to little avail. By the beginning of World War Two it was declared bankrupt. Needing a source of income, George rejoined the Navy and World War Two on base maintenance in various parts of the country. In 1942 he was posted to Lowestoft to work at the St Luke's Naval Hospital on Kirkley Cliff, where he was in charge of maintenance. He continued working for the R.N. until he was demobilized in 1949.

Afterwards he remained in the area, staying at various lodging–houses in the Kirkley and Pakefield areas. One of these was with the Perrides family who owned a boarding–house on Kirkley Cliff. Mr Perrides, a bewhiskered and erudite old gentleman, also ran the Kessingland pharmacy and he and George soon became fast friends as, amongst other things, they both liked a drink and a game of chess. Also, they shared a love of debate and would discuss anything and everything long into the night.

In a pub in the long–gone old Beach Village called the *East of England Tavern* George, in a chance conversation with local builder Owen Gray, was asked whether he would contract out some work. George, who had started up again as a painter and decorator, readily accepted. Knowing he had no permanent address Gray, in due course, offered him accommodation. It was a rather weird offer – a piece of waste ground in Pakefield Street with a collection of old tumbledown sheds and other buildings on it, including a very large greenhouse.

George spent some time adapting these old buildings to his needs and in due course moved into the largest one, making himself comfortable with a paraffin stove, an old bed, a Tilley lamp and various personal effects.

Working for Owen Gray meant that George was accumulating large amounts of old building materials. Selling them meant that he could modestly supplement his income. He also started selling second–hand furniture.

The 'Emporium' was constructed from anything and everything, with the plum tree still valiantly growing through the roof. The bric–a–brac accumulated and before long George found that he had built up a good trade in it.

The years passed and one day his board appeared outside as usual but now the words 'ESTABLISHED HERE THIRTY–FIVE YEARS' headed the list of services shown on it.

Although the board promised a multitude of different services, George took it considerably easier in later life and was fond of sitting outside on summers days, philosophizing with anyone who liked to stop and talk, while the old builders' handcart he had used since his earliest beginnings decayed sedately away tipped up on end against an outer wall, and in the milder seasons robins made their nests in its crevices.

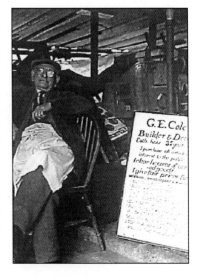

One service he did still offer was tool–sharpening. People would bring their blunt scissors, knives or garden tools and George, with his hand–operated grinder, would furnish them with a bright new edge.

As long as I had known George I had been curious about the meaning of the words ADJ No.174 written in red paint across the front doors of the building. As he lived at the back of this strange old place with no facilities, he feared that the authorities would ask him to leave so he made out that this place stood next to a house that he owned. He needn't have bothered.They knew about him and provided him with a key to the public toilet across the road, which enabled him to use it out of hours!

27

George continued in this way of life for several more years and died in the early 1980s at the age of eighty–nine, leaving a distinct gap in the community life of Pakefield. He was buried at Kirkley cemetery.

These days, passing the modern bungalow that now stands on that very site and reflecting on George, I sometimes wonder if his old sea friend ever collected the brass–bound leather trunk which George always said he was saving for him, the contents of which, to this day, remain a mystery or was it thrown away in clearance when he died, along with all his other possessions?

DICK 'MUCKO' SAUNDERS – 'THE MAN WITH THE POLE'

Dick Saunders was Lowestoft's town lamplighter for many years. Each evening as it grew dusk, carrying his lamplighter's pole, he would turn on and light every gas–lamp in the town and, even as Florence Nightingale was once known as 'The Lady with the Lamp', so was Dick Saunders known as 'The Man with the Pole'. As well as being town lamplighter he also ran a small coal yard in Whapload Road from where he conducted a round in the area.

Small in stature and sporting an enormous bushy beard, Saunders lived in one of the Scores. Probably owing to the nature of his work he sported a perpetually grimy appearance and as a consequence was nicknamed 'Mucko' by the locals. However, a devout Methodist and lay–preacher, when in church and dressed in his Sunday finery, the grime of his work washed off him, his appearance was altogether different and he looked quite a gentleman.

The boys of the town, when meeting Dick Saunders, would politely greet him with, "Good morning Mr Saunders," but when they were safely past, they would chant 'Old Mucko! Old Mucko!' At this, a stream of shouting would issue from the lamplighter's lips and he would give pursuit to the boys, thrusting the long pole he used for lighting the gas–lamps at their heels, at which they would nimbly jump and dodge. It all seemed little more than a bit of fun on either side.

But then these local boys decided to play a prank on him. They also acquired a long pole and one evening at dusk as Mucko walked round the town lighting the street lamps the boys, walking a distance behind, were extinguishing them. They must have been reported by someone for, when they returned to school, they were called to the Headmaster's office and each received six of the best!

One incident involving Mucko caused quite a stir in the town. A 'lunatic' (a good old–fashioned term but then this was the 1800s) escaped from the padded room in the Oulton Infirmary where he had been incarcerated. Making good his escape by climbing through the skylight on the roof, he began tearing off slates and hurling them at a group of men who were working below. The men ran for assistance and the escapee, clad in only his shirt, leapt to the ground, seized a chopper from somewhere and then, across the road, he spied Mucko's coal–cart with the owner sitting on board, Mucko having stopped to make a delivery.

With a blood–curdling cry the man, wielding the chopper, charged across the road and jumped on board the coal–cart. Poor Mucko, understandably terrified by this sight, quickly took refuge in a nearby tree. The man paused briefly for a few attempts at dislodging him from the tree by pelting him with lumps of coal then, tiring of this game, whipped the horse into action and drove furiously off down the town, flinging lumps of coal right and left as he went.

After a while the cart, completely out of control, crashed into a display stand outside a shop and overturned. The man, who was unhurt, sprang up, snatched up the chopper and, shaking off would–be captors, found himself at the door of the *Windsor Castle* pub, to which he attempted to gain entry.

He went to the door of the pub, tried it and found the door locked. It was not yet opening time. So wielding the chopper he blithely smashed it down! After gaining access in this somewhat unusual manner he strode over to the bar and swept it clear of glasses. A wild–eyed man wearing only a shirt suddenly confronted a rather shaken landlady. "Whatever do you want?" she stammered incredulously. "I want all your money and a pair of trousers," was the solemn reply.

At this point the landlady, with a sudden leap forward, grabbed him by the throat, pushing him backwards to the floor. A fierce struggle ensued and he broke away. Then officials, who had now tracked him down, arrived to take him back to the Infirmary but on seeing them he broke away and dived through the window – which was closed! On the ground outside he was eventually overpowered after a prolonged struggle and taken back to the Infirmary where he was placed in another padded cell. An hour later he was again missing and officials searched the whole area for an hour but to no avail. Later still he was found in the next room, fast asleep!

Mucko, who got his cart back in one piece, plus a traumatised old horse which he had to rest, managed to salvage some of his coal and after a while things gradually assumed a state of recovery.

Soon, headlines appeared in the local paper. Spectacularly entitled 'DANGEROUS LUNATIC AT LARGE WITH CHOPPER!' the local paper gave an exhaustive account of the escapee, his skirmish with Mucko and the landlady of the *Windsor Castle*. For a while it was the talk of the town. Mucko chuckled and said that it was one of the most exciting things that had happened to him in his life.

Soon the whole thing ceased to be topical and life went on much the same as before except now when the boys cheeked Mucko, and he lunged at him with his lamplighter's pole, they would dance around chanting, " Old Mucko, Old Mucko, dangerous lunatic at large with chopper!"

It was said that Mucko one day, gazing into an undertaker's parlour where a coffin was being made, wistfully remarked to a passer–by, "Please God, if I live long enough, I should like a coffin like that!" Dick Saunders was the town's lamplighter from 1850 till 1900 and departed from this world in 1910. I somehow can't help wondering whether he got the coffin of his choice!

'HAPPY' WELHAM

Alfred Welham, a large man with a red and bulbous nose, was, because of his jovial nature, nicknamed 'Happy' and lived in Lighthouse Score with his wife Phoebe. He earned a living in several different ways. One was carting the equipment of fishermen who had just landed from a fishing trip – oilskins, kitbags, boots and their owners – all for a tanner or a shilling a time, depending on how much they had.

 He did the same with the suitcases of newly arrived holidaymakers from the railway station and his trusty old donkey pulled the cart.

At some point or another he retired the donkey which was becoming rather old and feeble, and bought a little piebald pony but the donkey obviously meant a lot to him, for during one of the many floods experienced by the Beach Village, he took it to an upstairs bedroom for safety!

He might have been grateful to his animals for occasionally he would get so inebriated at the local pub after a night out that on leaving that cherished establishment and returning to his cart to go home, he was incapable of driving. His little terrier dog Blot, which travelled everywhere with him, would take the reins and guide the cart to the other end of Whapload Road. The donkey knew the way home and together the two of them would ferry Happy home in his inebriated state.

In the summer Happy and his wife (who all the children called Aunt Phoebe) ran a number of enterprises on the beach. She made ginger beer and lemonade in their kitchen and there would be buckets, bottles and all sorts of other equipment for the making of these beverages. She would tie down the stoppers of the old stone jars for maximum fizz and explosions in their kitchen were said to be not infrequent! Happy would put a notice above his kitchen door which read: 'If you're dry come in and try Happy's homemade drink!' The lemonade was sold for a halfpenny a bottle, as was a home–made wine also made by Phoebe in their kitchen.

A large proportion of Happy's working time was spent as a chimney–sweep therefore his appearance was almost always rather grimy. Someone once said of him, "He never did wash – only if it rained." When he was at work groups of children would gather to see the brush emerge from the chimney–pot. Occasionally he would misjudge the length of rod required and add too many lengths, pushing the brush up so far that it hung down in an arc, touching the tiles of the roof, much to the amusement of both children and passers–by. On one particular occasion, however, he got into quite a predicament. He was sweeping the chimney of a cottage owned by two old ladies who shared the children's fascination for watching the brush emerge, and had gone outside to see the spectacle.

A while passed and despite constant thrusting on Happy's part and his adding rod after rod to the length of the sweep's brush, and growing more and more puffed and red in the face, the head of the brush steadfastly refused to emerge. The old ladies waited patiently in the garden.

At length, the reason for the delay was discovered. In the process of sweeping the chimney, Happy had somehow dislodged a brick from the lining. This had caused the brush to follow through as Happy pushed and, as he added more lengths of rod, the brush travelled further up the back of the loft. A local builder had to be called in and he had no option but to cut a hole in the loft in order to release the brushes, which had jammed solid!

Another amusing incident occurred when Happy, for reasons best known to himself, decided to clear a customer's chimney by using gunpowder. In those days this was sometimes used as a quick and easy method, cheaper than calling in the sweep but regarded as a bit dangerous. It certainly would not have complied with modern health and safety regulations! Happy, it seems, was not used to employing this method but on this occasion thought it a desirable short cut.

Having obtained the gunpowder, which could then be bought from any hardware store, he threw it inside a wall–stove and quickly shut the stove door. The result was a huge explosion; the stove door blasted open, dumping a large amount of the soot from the chimney into the kitchen. It seems that he made two mistakes. One was to employ far too much explosive; the other was that he should quickly have run a cane rod up the chimney so that some of the blast could dissipate. At any rate, it cost Happy a lot of cleaning up and repairs, and I think it safe to say that he never repeated the experiment!

During the First World War when the German navy bombarded the town, a shell unexpectedly fell in Lighthouse Score, near to Happy's house. Never one to pass up the chance of making a few bob, Happy grabbed a broom, rolled the shell into his garden, and charged passers–by twopence to see the 'new exhibit'. After a while, the Navy came with a lorry and took it away, by which time Happy had made himself precisely one shilling.

Although at one point he told friends and neighbours that he had retired, he still carried on much the same as before. Someone asked him how it was possible to distinguish between his retirement and when he was working. "Well," chuckled Happy, "You see all these flowers I'm growing – dahlias, sunflowers, pansies and the like. Well, I never grew'em before I retired and now I do. That's how yer know!"

The flowers were a welcome addition to the area, adding a splash of colour. Happy concentrated on growing them and his cart was often full of their nodding heads as he passed through the town, on his way to sell them to this place or that; Blot, the terrier, sitting up beside him as he always did. Happy would take most of these to his wife's stall on the South Beach and place them in buckets containing water amongst where she sold her lemonade and coconut–ice (made to secret recipes), beach pails, little home–made windmills and almost anything else one might need or desire on the beach.

Happy and his wife continued on for several more years, until one winter when people noticed that they hadn't been seen for quite some time. The alarm was raised; two men fetched a ladder and gained access to the cottage. Happy and his wife were found in bed, almost dead with influenza. They were taken to hospital, but Happy died soon after. Phoebe, however, survived this episode and continued to live at their cottage for a good number of years to come – in fact, well after the Second World War. Happy died in the late 1930s, having lived in the fishermen's cottages at Lighthouse Score for most of his life, for thirty years even before 1900 – a real old Beachman!

'THE REDOUBTABLE CHARLOTTE AGAIN'!
THE STORY OF CHARLOTTE HIGH

Little can be known about the early life of Charlotte High, only the briefest mention of her being recorded in the 1881 census, and this tells us only that she was born in Pakefield in 1847.

As she first appears in local papers with the surname High, her married name, there really can be no clue as to her early origins. We must therefore assume that she was born into the small but thriving fishing community which existed in Pakefield, went to the local elementary school (she could well have attended the Cunningham School, which was situated near to Pakefield Church and one of the first elementary schools for the poor in the area).

On leaving, she would have most probably have worked in some capacity in the fishing industry. So life for Charlotte would have been quite similar to that of other young girls of her time and environment. However, all this changed irreconcilably when she met and married George High.

An insatiable appetite for drinking and gambling meant that George spent what little money they had on fuelling his addictions. They went to live in Lowestoft and Charlotte also began to drink, and eventually turned to prostitution as a means of funding her (and George's) drinking habits. Alcohol seemed to bring out a violent streak in her and she started to amass a string of convictions for drunkenness and for soliciting, as well as various violent acts, as did her two companions, Susannah Lane and Charity Felgate. When the three of them were run in together for drunken and riotous behaviour, they caused so much noise and disruption that they had to be put in separate cells. Charlotte then proceeded to smash up her cell, breaking a bench, a washbowl and anything else she could lay hands on, to smithereens. When she eventually calmed down and slept off the effects of the drink, she was fined one pound and made to pay compensation to the police for the damage she had caused.

She continued to be, in the words of one judge, 'the pest of the neighbourhood', causing mayhem everywhere she went. Charlotte and her cronies were frequently the root cause of a fair percentage of petty crime in the Lowestoft area and, as Charlotte seemed to be the ringleader, she tended to elicit more severe penalties than did the others, which probably had more to do with Charlotte's reputation than with actual justice. For instance, when the three of them were run in for using 'bad language on the promenade' Charlotte was fined one pound, whereas the penalty for her two confederates for the same crime was only ten shillings.

Her name became familiar in the local newspapers and the Lowestoft Journal, after reporting innumerable court appearance by Charlotte, headed this particular one 'The Redoubtable Charlotte Again!' which is where the title for

this feature originates from. The paper covers a case whereby Charlotte is appearing in court yet again, this time for stealing from a shop. At this point she appears in the witness box wearing, in the words of one observer, 'a most bizarre costume'. No actual description is given of her attire but it is a wonderful exercise for the imagination to speculate on how she might have looked!

Once in the dock she turned to the Bench and appealed for leniency. "Don't be too hard–hearted," said Charlotte, looking at the Chairman. "Remember that you have children and you wouldn't want their parent's hairs (heirs) come down with sorrow from the grave." At this strange and incomprehensible outburst there was an eruption of mirth throughout the court. Mr Harvey, the Chairman, adjourned the case, exclaiming that under the circumstances a fair hearing was impossible. Charlotte was led down to the cells and searched, whereupon knife blades were found concealed inside the lining of her coat. She was detained, pending a further hearing. Miraculously, after a few days someone came up with the money for her bail and she was released.

A serial offender, it wasn't long before Charlotte found herself in court again, for soliciting in public. With her were her old partners in crime, Susannah Lane and Charity Felgate. They were all found guilty and the other two fined but Charlotte, in breach of her bail, was given a prison sentence of three months. After the hearing she was duly taken down to the cells and incarcerated. Throughout the proceedings she had been unusually quiet and subdued. Early that evening when the prison warder went to check on her she was sleeping but on a later check he found her hanging by the neck from the bars of her cell. The alarm was raised and Charlotte, who had almost succeeded in taking her own life, was taken to the prison hospital and revived.

Charlotte's attempted suicide, her bizarre behaviour and her alcoholism lead the authorities to decide that she might benefit by finishing her current sentence at the local lunatic asylum, where she was accordingly sent for 'a period of correction and guidance'.

When released from the lunatic asylum Charlotte was soon back on the streets again, plying her trade. Some avoided her, knowing she had been an inmate at the local lunatic asylum, as any manifest psychological problem in those days was taboo and frightening. On the other hand, some men actively sought her 'company' because the dark and mysterious side of all this appealed to the more obscure aspects of their own natures. Charlotte seemed to revel in the charisma and sense of power that her newly–found official lunacy seemed to give her and her costumes became yet more bizarre, and her turn of phrase yet more lurid.

Prostitutes, by nature of their profession, have few friends; the prostitutes of a town usually stay together to guard one another against being beaten up, raped, robbed or even murdered – and these were no exception. There was also considerable competition between them – each vying to attract the most clientele. It is not clear who usually won, but what is known is that the drunks who inhabited the seedy pubs of the area constantly used them for their sexual gratification, their fee being probably not much more than the price of perpetual drunkenness – a mercenary life indeed!

Then an incident occurred that totally changed life for Charlotte. A policeman on night duty was found lying unconscious near the *Suffolk Hotel*, having received a stab wound to the neck. Constable Allen Brooks Chapman was taken to the local hospital where he soon recovered consciousness. Two circumstantial factors led the police to arrest Charlotte and bring her in for questioning. One was that she was known to have an intense hatred of the police; the other factor was that she was frequently known to carry knife blades, one of which was found at the scene. When arrested, Charlotte readily admitted guilt, exclaiming, "Did I kill him? It was my avowed intent!" She was taken off to the cells, this time to await trial for attempted murder.

Mr W.H. Clubbe, surgeon, said he examined Chapman (who fortunately soon regained consciousness when in hospital) and found him to have received a wound about two inches below his right ear, very near to the large blood vessels of the neck. The wound as it was did not constitute a danger but it was only good fortune that the knife had not struck an artery; if it had it done so the consequences for Chapman might have been very serious indeed. As things were, the wound was quite severe and it would be some time before he would be able to resume work. The wound, said Mr Clubbe, was definitely of the same shape as the blade of the knife found on Charlotte High. Lydia Batley said that High purchased the knife from her for one shilling.

Inspector Jefferies said that he went to the prisoner's cell on Saturday evening and, after having issued her with a caution, told her he would have to charge her with stabbing P.C. Chapman. "Is he dead?" asked High. "If I had had a razor I would have cut off his whole head!" She further added, "I do it out of pure love for him." (Ripple of laughter from the gallery). She was the worse for drink and said that she had had her revenge.

The charge was then read over to the defendant and High was asked what she had to say in her defence but would give no direct answer. Eventually the chairman conceded that under the circumstances it was his painful duty to commit her to the next Assizes for the attempted murder of P.C. Allen Brooks Chapman. The prisoner was then led back to the cells.

The Assizes having assembled Charlotte was indicted for the attempted murder of P.C. Allen Brooks Chapman on Sept 8th where, with the same expectant faces lining the gallery, a second count charged her with wounding with intent to disable and a third pointed to intent to commit grievous bodily harm, causing a murmur to run through the general assembly and at which Charlotte fainted.

After a delay she recovered and proceeded to plead not guilty, admitting stabbing the officer, but stressing that she had not intended to kill him. She urged that she had had 'great occasion to exact revenge on him' adding, "He knocked me about so much and I bear the marks now. The knife made an impression which I could not have made had I merely struck him. Hardly anyone on earth knows what I am suffering because of him." The Commissioner interpreted these remarks as a change to a plea of not guilty and the case proceeded accordingly. Mr Wreufordaley watched the case on the prisoner's behalf.

Presently the prisoner fainted again, causing yet another delay. She was examined by Mr Clubbe, surgeon, who thought she would be able to endure the rest of the trial. Constable Allen Brooks Chapman again gave evidence, "I am a Police Constable stationed at Lowestoft. On the evening of Sept 8th I spoke to the prisoner and told her to moderate her language. I was standing near to the *Suffolk Hotel* at the time she appeared. She was obviously drunk and using very bad language. When I asked her to move she became even more abusive and her language became worse than ever. I said just go home and be quiet. She replied, 'You b****! You have taken out a summons against me today. I will stab you to the b**** heart!'"

She then went away along Denmark Road and out of sight. Chapman added that after completing a beat he was again standing by the *Suffolk Hotel* when he heard shouting and coarse language being used. Then Charlotte High came round the corner, approached him again and complained that some men had been interfering with her. Chapman's response to this was to tell her to go home and be quiet, as at home there would be no men to interfere with her.

About fifteen minutes after this Chapman said P.C. Snell had joined him and they stood together talking, when he suddenly felt a blow to his neck. "I put my hand up and there was blood running down. Shortly afterwards I lost consciousness." P.C Snell said he saw the prisoner making off down the road and promptly arrested her. Suddenly, a squawking voice from the dock, "I do not care; I have had my revenge, and do what you like with me. I don't care, then or now. I have always been knocked about. You are all right now that you have got me, aren't you! I want the chance to speak but I don't get it. I wish I were dead, and then we would all be all right." (Ripple of laughter from the gallery).The Chair dryly remarked that she would have every chance to speak if she would only be quiet.

William Harvey, a railwayman living in Lowestoft, was next to give evidence. He stated, "On that Saturday night at about eleven o'clock I was standing in the vicinity of the *Suffolk Hotel*. A policeman was there and the defendant was screaming something to him about men who would not leave her alone. As she was walking towards the policeman she saw me and said, 'My God, you!' Another policeman soon joined the first and they stood together talking. High returned and, sidling up to the policeman, suddenly made a striking motion to his head. At first I thought she was going to knock off his helmet but when he fell down I realised that something far more serious had taken place. Then I went over to see what the matter was and he lay unconscious. I got him to the hospital while the other constable arrested High."

Ann Jefferies, wife of Inspector Jefferies, said she had searched High on her arrest at about twenty to twelve on the night the incident occurred and had found a large pocket–knife. On this were bloodstains, which remained. (At this point, she held up the knife). When challenged with this she had said, "I am only sorry I did not cut off his head."

P.C. Brooks Chapman, the injured policeman, was next to give evidence. "She was using foul language," said the constable, "and I told her to go home, upon which she replied, 'You have taken out a summons against me today and I will stab you to the heart!' With this she went off, walking along Denmark Road. The next thing I knew was a stabbing sensation in my neck, before I passed out. I woke up in the hospital. High was drunk at the time and that was why I had taken out a summons against her. I have known the prisoner for about ten months and in this time I have helped take her to the station about three times but have spoken to her about thirty. I have no particular quarrel with her and most certainly have never inflicted upon her any form of violence, including the damage to her ankle which she claims I am responsible for. I recently pushed her off the bridge because she was using bad language but this certainly did not involve the use of excessive force."

Summing up, the learned Chairman said, "Charlotte High, you are here before the court today for a very serious offence indeed, that of the attempted murder of a police officer; namely Allen Brooks Chapman. It can be readily observed that the vicious course of your life and also an intense hatred of the police have lead to your appearance here today. You not long ago attempted to commit suicide, whereby a spell of treatment coupled with the absence of drink brought you back to a healthful state of mind; now you have reverted to the kind of life which has ended in your present circumstance. As for your children, I cannot see what benefit a person of your style of life could ever be to them."

Charlotte replied, "I have been unfortunate, still justice ought to be done to me. Five months ago Chapman put my foot out and nothing was said about that. That was a serious matter as well. Mr Clubbe saw me in hospital and it was months before I could move in bed. This Chapman did and he knows it and he has often said that he would shake the living daylights out of me."

In the summing–up the court found Charlotte High guilty and she was given the somewhat lenient sentence, considering the severity of the crime, of nine month's hard labour. Had the officer died, of course, things would have been very different, and she would no doubt have been executed for murder. As it was, Charlotte, after serving her sentence, moved to Norwich – doubtless much to the relief of the legal worthies of Lowestoft – and although she probably carried on in much the same old way, for us here in Lowestoft her story reaches a natural conclusion.

E.J. SINGLETON–SMITH

In about 1895 there came to live in Lowestoft a man who turned out to be one of the most colourful, enigmatic and eccentric school Headmasters in the area. Answering an advertisement for the post of Headmaster E.J. Singleton Smith took up at St Margaret's College, a boys' school in the town, and delighted his charges both with his penchant for drama and the arts, and also his general eccentricity and his approach to nature, especially to Entomology; one of his great loves. For reasons of brevity, I will refer to him as E.J.

E.J. sported a huge handlebar moustache with waxed ends, a large Roman nose, and was almost always clad in heavy jungle boots, a blue serge suit and a tie of 'vivid hue'. With a gesticulating, theatrical manner and an upper–class accent, he cut a striking and larger–than–life figure. Also, on his field excursions he often wore a pith–helmet as this, in his view, was the 'best way to protect the head in adverse circumstances'.

E.J. believed in getting the boys involved as much as possible; they loved the nature–walks he conducted and also the dramatic productions staged by the school, in which they participated. Ahead of his time in some respects, E.J.'s view was that the stimulus of personal involvement was the best way for schoolchildren to learn many things. He realised that Shakespeare, for example, had little impact if encountered only by studying text and learning quotes. The same, he considered, applied to Nature Studies and Biology. His methods proved popular. One boy wrote in his diary that he had not realised that being at school could actually be enjoyable until E.J. took over the school!

The Public Hall was conveniently situated next door but one. Of its many uses one was as a theatre and it was here that E.J. staged the various productions in which the boys participated.

Smith's entomological activities however took place largely on school holidays and at weekends and at night, and were unaccompanied. 'Wooed by insects, moths and solitude' he journeyed across the countryside with his nets and specimen boxes, to capture whatever species he regarded as rare and/or unusual, be it moth, butterfly, bird or animal. His special interest, however, was *microlepidoptera* (or small moths).

He attributed his interest in natural things to an incident in his childhood when he had received as a present a butterfly–net. The handle was twice as long as he was tall and, "I found I could also catch tadpoles and all sorts of other fascinating creatures from ponds with it, which proved a real bonus!" That day however he was out across the meadows, excitedly pursuing butterflies, spotted what turned out to be a Peacock butterfly, and gave chase.

The chase took him to what he described as a 'gentleman's park' which was fenced off. The butterfly flew over the fence and E.J., not to be discouraged, climbed over in pursuit. The butterfly lighted in the middle of a beautiful bed of flowers and he was reaching in after it when the owner of the park turned up, looking astonished. E.J. steeled himself to face the consequences, emerged from the shrubbery, confronted the owner and told him what he was doing was for a project at school. The owner, on seeing that it was a small boy that he was dealing with, and being impressed that he could know so much of the habits of moths and butterflies, told him that he could go there at any time. "At that early point," said E.J., "I learned that audacity can often be a trump card to naturalists."

In later life this proved to be true on more than one occasion. His hobby as a naturalist quite often led him to trespass on private land, and often he had to pit his wits to get him out of awkward corners. A good example of the latter was when he came up against a gamekeeper on the lands of a certain wealthy peer whilst searching for the nest of a golden–crested wren. "I suppose you've got leave to come here?" the gamekeeper said officiously, "There's eggs about you know." "Yes, leave most certainly," replied E.J., "and eggs do not tempt me. I am pleased to see you so vigilant and I will most certainly inform his Lordship when I get back to the Hall." "Thank you most kindly," replied the gamekeeper, who was much flattered.

In the course of a night he would sometimes cover an incredible fifteen miles radius in his wanderings, snatching odd hours of sleep under hedgerows as he went, and travelling miles back to his home after the sun had risen. Referring to his time spent sleeping under hedgerows, E.J. would quote the Norfolk naturalist, Thomas Edwards, who shared similar experiences and said in his biography 'rats and stoats nosed around me'.

Ranging over the marshes he would seek out a friend, a fellow naturalist who lived on the river in a houseboat called 'Moorhen' – a welcome respite from a no doubt fatiguing journey. Throwing his nets and other equipment onto the deck he would ease himself gently into the cabin and there would partake of supper (the friend introduced him to jellied eels and since he had developed a partiality for them), and the two of them would gossip for hours over the tea–table. E.J. spent several days at a time as a guest aboard the boat, waking early to experience the river by daylight and spending time with the friend on excursions over the marshes. The two would separate at some point and, when the evening came, would meet back at the boat and compare notes over supper.

Not being able to carry all his specimens and equipment home he would leave various tins, boxes and jars at appointed places along his route, to be collected later. Some of them, if he had left them too long, would be putrefied on his return and therefore absolutely useless as specimens!

His room, situated at one end of the school, was what could only be (and probably often was) described as 'chaotic'. Festooned with books, telescopes, cameras, specimen cases and all the paraphernalia required to hunt butterflies and other insects, there were so many possessions that he had his bed built up off the floor in 'bunk style' to allow him to store various items underneath it. There was a desk where he wrote; at a younger age he had been an ambitious young writer and became a great friend of Matthew Arnold. He spent years at this desk in his room at the school, snatching a spare hour here and there, to write a novel which never saw the light of day.

One day, quite without warning, fire broke out at the Public Hall. The cause of the fire remains unknown but must have caused E.J. some anxiety, as this was where he housed his extensive (and lifelong) butterfly and moth collection.

After a concerted attempt by E.J. and others the collection was saved, and temporarily moved to the Victoria Arcade, which stood opposite. Smith, in his relief at being able to salvage the whole collection, gave his pupils three day's special holiday.

The collection eventually found its way to the Public Library in Suffolk Road and remained there until the new library was instated in Clapham Road in the early 1980s. As for the Public Hall the fire was put out quite quickly but part of the stage and other areas inside were badly damaged by the fire. The neighbouring buildings, including St Margaret's, were unscathed, as was the nearby Insurance Office, which specialised in fire protection!

The fire certainly caused a setback to the new play which the school was rehearsing but as they say 'the show must go on'. They decided to stage it at St Margaret's College which had a stage, albeit a rather smaller one. Damaged scenery had to be reconstructed and the whole thing scaled down to accommodate the smaller stage. Everyone lent a hand.

Not everyone shared E.J.'s enthusiasm for nature. He was born in Chobham, Surrey, where he attended school, leaving with enough qualifications to take up a teaching post as Assistant Master at another school. Here, he felt himself, a young man with an enthusiasm for learning, to be little more than 'a warder in a prison'. Realising that he needed to increase the scope of his knowledge in order to improve his position and take up more interesting work, he saved 'by strictly parsimonious habit' enough money to enable him to study at Durham University, where he read English Literature.

Whilst at Durham he still avidly pursued his hobby as a naturalist. ('Moth–fiends, like bird–men are born,' he once observed.) Noticing that his fellow students seemed largely oblivious to nature he attempted to introduce some of them to its wonders but, he said, was pitched into the river for his pains and had rapidly to get back into the boat he was using, to stop himself sinking into the mud. "When I got back on land I was covered in feculent slime," remarked E.J. This, he said, was one of the worst experiences he had ever encountered as a naturalist and he never came to understand why apparently intelligent people at a University should behave in this manner. Undaunted, however, he continued to pursue his hobby with vigour and enthusiasm, encountering all kinds of strange happenings on the way.

One such was when he was staying, as he put it, 'within railway distance of some extensive oak woods'. At the woods there were reported sightings of the Purple Emperor moth and it was of this creature that E.J. desired a sighting. Knowing that it was a species which tended to fly high but descended to 'feed up on putrid substances' he boarded the train, carrying with him in an old leather bag a dead crow, a dead cat and some mackerel – all of which stank to high heaven – call this dedication if you will! E.J. duly took a seat in one of the carriages. Before long a 'portly gentleman' entered – and a woman to match! Sitting opposite Smith, their noses began to twitch and the man, pulling down the window of the carriage, asked E.J. if he could 'smell an unholy aroma'. When Smith replied that he could not the man replied, "I feel sorry for you, then!" and, along with his wife, stormed out of the carriage. Presently, another couple replaced the recently departed one and much the same scenario took place, except that this time, on being told that he could smell nothing, this man stormed out, "... with a picturesque description of my nasal organ; which ..." and here E.J. indicated his large Roman nose, "... as you will perceive, is no mean one!"

Amongst other things, E.J. became well–known in Lowestoft for his moth and butterfly hunting ventures. With his long–handled net he would pursue his quarry round the street–lamps when need be, running fast in pursuit on bandy legs, long–handled net at the ready.

Sometimes quite a chase could ensue before he landed a quarry. On one occasion a man shinned up a lamp–post to assist him with a capture, on yet another a friendly policeman lent a hand. Young girls would beg him to 'have a go' with his net and generally speaking the public seemed to see it all as great fun!

During his time at Lowestoft he collected many different types of moth around the lamp–posts, for example in 1923 he amassed a total of 117 different species. I cannot help reflecting that in these days of pesticides and general pollution, the street–lamps of Lowestoft would yield nothing like that number! Smith's favourite haunt in the town was Belle Vue Park, where he did much of his collecting.

He also used 'live cages'. These were mostly whisky–boxes converted for the purpose and trapped moths by attracting them with lights placed inside. Smith would place them at strategic points around the area, at times enlisting the help of his pupils to collect them up at the end of a session.

Another thing E.J. would do was to collect large quantities of moth and butterfly chrysalids and place them in his room in open–topped boxes. At times many would escape from their pupae–cases, and could be seen by passers–by pouring out of the windows!

In the meantime there was his work as a Headmaster which, of course, occupied a great deal of his time and also his work in amateur theatre. When the fire broke out at the Public Hall the school were working on a production of 'The Death of General Gordon', with E.J. of course as producer. As already stated, the fire caused a major setback, with many items having to be reconstructed or replaced. In this case E.J. was also the obvious candidate to be cast in the leading role. He was a busy man!

Once, E.J. joined the ranks of the supernatural – at least in the perceptions of a local gamekeeper! This came about as follows: E.J. was in a wooded copse at Barnby, endeavouring to catch an *Essex Emeraldgeometra,* a species hitherto captured only in Norfolk but which had recently been sighted in this area. Reaching what he regarded as an appropriate spot, he lay down stock still in the undergrowth, holding his net across him, after first covering his face with phosphorus (which I suppose was employed to attract the moths!)

After some time his endeavours were rewarded and a specimen appeared, flying toward him. With a characteristic sweeping movement, it was secured in the net. E.J., mightily pleased, made sure the moth was filed away securely, rose and started back the way he had come. On the way he encountered the gamekeeper coming in the opposite direction. The gamekeeper let out a frightened yell and fled back to the lodge, where he bolted himself securely in. "He went as if Mephistopheles himself was after him," chuckled E.J.

Absent–minded at times, he had neglected to clean the phosphorus off his face, which still gave off an unearthly effervescence. Later the gamekeeper reported the incident to the local press, claiming that he had encountered the Barnby ghost! As if the whole scenario did not already contain enough humour, the office of the Lowestoft Journal happened to be situated in the basement beneath St Margaret's College!

E.J. died suddenly at St Margaret's College in the winter of 1926. In his thirty–one years as Headmaster he had made countless friends and acquaintances in Lowestoft and beyond and many of these attended the funeral service. A literary colleague at the school in a speech at the funeral service likened him to Victor Hugo's description of Gilliat: 'rarely seen with a gun, but oft with a net'. Indeed, in his time at St Margaret's E.J. collected a staggering total of 325 different species of moths and butterflies; his lifetime collection totalled many more. A well as these he had collected many specimens of other natural phenomena such as various stuffed birds and animals and several fossils.

E.J. was acclaimed as an inspired and colourful Headmaster who tried to encourage staff and pupils alike to participate in school activities and to share in his love of nature, and when he died it was seen as the end of an era. The Public Hall was never rebuilt after the fire and so naturally was not used again. E.J. had put its facilities to good use and by the time of his death had worked with his staff and pupils to stage many productions there. St Margaret's School for Boys carried on, this time with a Mr Tungate at the helm until, in 1941, wartime bombs destroyed the whole block.

GEORGE ATKINSON

Some time in 1911, a young reporter visited a large house on Wellington Esplanade where George Atkinson, a renowned Natural Scientist, now lived and worked. As the young reporter entered, the kitchen was full of smoke and Atkinson, elderly, excitable, gesticulated wildly through it, asking the young reporter if he would share his breakfast. "It's squid," he exclaimed, "cooked in its own ink. Wonderful!" He tipped the black, oily, pungent–smelling liquid onto a plate and began to eat with relish. Not surprisingly, the young reporter declined, instead settling for toast and some tea. "You youngsters won't live long on that sort of breakfast," commented Atkinson between mouthfuls of squid. "Have you ever tried bladder–wrack?" The young reporter had not. "Well, don't then," guffawed Atkinson. "It's bloody terrible. Tastes like sort of fishy rubber, yer know!"

George Atkinson, a brilliant scholar, was born in 1881 and read Zoology at Cambridge, where he gained a first. On leaving in 1904 he studied under and worked for one Dr Ganstrang, an eminent German biologist, and his team of scientists.

They travelled extensively in Britain, calling into various fishing ports such as Hull and Grimsby, and also abroad, investigating various marine phenomena; diving extensively to in vestigate the strange life which lie in and around deep–sea wrecks and the young George, in his own words, was introduced to a 'world of strange and wonderful things'.

Returning to England, he left the auspices of Dr Ganstrang in 1910 to join the newly–formed Ministry of Agriculture and Fisheries at their H.Q. in London.

He was frequently on assignments to Lowestoft; it was one of the places in the British Isles which had a prevalent fishing industry but of these many fishing ports it was Lowestoft with which Atkinson fell in love. After a few years (to Atkinson's delight) the Ministry bought and converted the Empire Hotel in Pakefield to a research laboratory and Atkinson, who now lived and worked permanently in Lowestoft, purchased a house on the Esplanade. It was from here that the young reporter was attempting to conduct his interview.

The reporter had visited George for the express purpose of sounding out his knowledge and expertise, in order to produce a report for the local newspaper for which he worked, about the current state of fishing in a typical English fishing town, particularly as George had conducted investigations into many other ports.

George Atkinson talked extensively and excitedly, as was his way, telling this tale and that until the young reporter, lacking experience in interview technique, realised that time had become short and, so far, Atkinson had talked of everything except the subject he had come to interview him on. Somehow, the reporter had to focus Atkinson to the subject for which he was interviewing him and presently said, "Mr. Atkinson, I came here to ask you what you considered to be the current state of the fishing industry in Britain today."

Atkinson considered for a while before making this simple statement, "My boy," said he, "Fishing is very like potato farming. If a farmer continues to harvest potatoes and plants none, the result will soon be no potatoes. That is the current state of fishing in Britain." He made no further comment. The young reporter saw that all he would get from Atkinson, at least for now, was flippancy and bid his farewells, feeling he had wasted his time in this instance but had met a pretty interesting man.

The next meeting between Atkinson and the young reporter took place some weeks later. As the latter strolled over Lowestoft Bridge, he was suddenly greeted by a booming voice, "Hey there – come and see what I've got!" It was Atkinson, perched on an archaic bicycle with solid tyres. A bucket dangled from the handlebars. "Come and see what we've got at the boating–pool!" He pedalled off furiously over the bridge in his excitement.

When the reporter arrived at the Esplanade boating–pool a strange sight greeted him. No boats sailed there today but the pool was full of fish which swam, flat and dun–coloured, against the blue of the bottom, doing their best to make themselves invisible.

As he watched, a boy dressed in boy–scouts uniform came from somewhere and tipped in a bag of salt. "See," exclaimed Atkinson excitedly, "Everyone can now study plaice in their own environment and learn their little secrets!" That morning the area around the boating–pool was a hive of activity. Atkinson had somewhere found a supply of live plaice and had paid the local scout troop to help him transfer them to the boating pool. He had then had them add bags of sea–salt to the water, to create a more life–supporting environment for the fish.

Increasingly intrigued by the man's eccentricity, the young reporter thought, "God, this will make a far more interesting story about our Mr. Atkinson!" and got out his notebook. He was right. It did make an interesting story. So did the second part of it. In the evening when everyone had gone, the scouts (and possibly other small boys) thought that these fish would be better 'studied' from the point of view of a frying–pan and, creeping back to the pool armed with nets, cleaned out every last one, bringing Atkinson's project to an abrupt halt!

When he decided to retire from the Ministry, George Atkinson had been in Lowestoft for many years. Known to the people here as the town's eccentric scientist and respected for his knowledge, he was always dreaming up projects and experiments, in which he would often encourage the townsfolk to participate.

He gave a party for the town's dignitaries, which was staged at the *Suffolk Hotel*, and in an after–dinner speech he said that he had enjoyed his working life and being based in Lowestoft. He spoke of how well he had been treated in Lowestoft – 'some of the nicest folks anywhere' – and the interest with which they had responded to his desire to get people participating in science. With this he said, "We had ice–cream with the meal tonight – here's what it was made of," and produced a string of herring and a length of seaweed! In the case of most people this would have been taken for granted to be a hoax but in the case of Mr. Atkinson, somewhat less so.

Atkinson's comment to the reporter on the state of the fishing industry had been over–simplistic and flippant but obviously he had a scientist's insight into the direction things would eventually take and of course he would be proved to be right.

On retirement, George Atkinson moved to a small aquatic institute run by the American government where, due to his extensive knowledge in his subject, he was employed as Research Advisor. This suited him admirably as George, although he loved Lowestoft, grew to detest the cold British winters and there, as far as I know, he spent the rest of his life.

FRED MURRAY

In the early 1980s a busker appeared overnight it seemed in Lowestoft, and positioned himself outside W.H. Smiths in London Road North. Greeted at first with surprise and possibly suspicion (who was the long–haired man complete with guitar, who had appeared apparently from nowhere, to play music to the Lowestoft public?) but after a while he became a familiar sight. He played away doggedly through the days, strumming his guitar and playing harmonica, his cord cap by his feet to receive any coins that appreciative members of the public might wish to contribute.

A tall man in his thirties, usually smart looking in his white jacket and jeans, Fred's electric guitar sported a small amplifier powered by a motor–cycle battery which he would periodically take to a local garage to have charged. His equipment also included something probably known better to musicians than to the rest of the population – namely a 'wah–wah pedal'. This is a 'pitch–bender' of sorts. Plugged into the rest of the equipment, worked by a foot–pedal, they produce a characteristic 'wow wow wow' effect when applied. Jimi Hendrix frequently used them in his music, as did many other famous guitarists of the rock world – and Fred used his in his music with frequent emphasis – as some people may remember!

Born in London in the 1950s, Fred left a grammar school without many qualifications, "I was good at English and music – and that's it," said he.

Casting around for what to do by way of a career (including taking the Civil Service examination), Fred soon decided that the best and nicest way to make a living would be to simply carry on playing the guitar. He had been playing from an early age. Honing his skills, he made sure he was as good as most other people and could play almost any style. His first paid gigs were in pubs as a one–man act where he played folk/blues, basing himself on his idol Bob Dylan, and playing acoustic style.

After a while doing this, he decided to extend his repertoire and began visiting various London clubs, now deciding to go electric. The jazz clubs were the places where serious musicians hung out and where some of the worthies, who later became famous by branching out into rock, cut their teeth. Fred became a regular at several of these, filling in for anyone who was short of a guitarist. He would also play bass when required and in the end he was playing both jazz and rock and becoming well–known around the club circuit.

Eventually a band who later shot to fame offered him a permanent place in their band with a view to an impending recording contract and, had he taken it, Fred would have found himself very rich and successful but he was growing increasingly disillusioned with the London music scene and its excesses and felt that although it was offering him something in one respect, it was stifling his creative talent in another. By the summer of 1976 he had quit the scene, and was hitch–hiking across Britain with a guitar on his back, a free man once again.

Drifting across Britain and living from the proceeds of his playing, Fred managed to see most of our Fair Isles and claimed that he had a more enjoyable time than he ever had when on the London music scene, and feeling far more relaxed. Altogether, he was on the road for nearly five years, and his wanderings included crossing over to the Continent and playing in France and Italy. At any rate, one day in 1981 he arrived in Lowestoft, and ended up staying for several years. According to Fred he had not intended to stay more than the usual few days that he stayed anywhere but perhaps by this time he felt an inherent need to settle and said he found the people of Lowestoft more generous than in many of the towns in which he had busked. So, one way and another, he ended up staying in Lowestoft.

Summer and winter, Fred slept under one or the other of the piers. He cherished his independence, saying that he did not wish to be beholden to a landlord. Apparently, he would dig a hole in the sand and shingle under the pier, and then line it with ground–sheeting to guard against the damp, using a heavy–duty military sleeping–bag to keep out the cold. In extreme conditions, however, he would concede to occasionally staying with friends. He was said to be an accomplished chess player so perhaps passed these cold times playing chess with some of these friends at their homes.

In the halcyon days when a cigarette could actually be enjoyed in a public place without fear of retribution, Fred could often be seen in Took's Bakery taking a break from street entertaining and indulging in a coffee and a roll–up. He had a bike and could sometimes be seen in 'off–duty' moments going from place to place.

Fred was something of an enigma to most people. He was a familiar sight in the town but people knew little about him. He was the man who had suddenly turned up in the streets with a guitar to play them a rich mixture of rhythm and blues, rock and folk, but always kept himself very much to himself. Then one day this man who by now the locals had come to regard as a permanent feature of the town, vanished as suddenly as he had come. To this day, no–one knows for sure where he went or why; he had said nothing of his plans to anyone but Fred was naturally a drifter and perhaps once again felt the need to travel and broaden his horizons, and give some other town the benefit of his talents.